Quick-Change Quilts

12 QUILTS FROM 6 PATTERNS

Terri Nussbaum

Martingale™
& COMPANY

That Patchwork Place® is an imprint of
Martingale & Company™.

Quick-Change Quilts: 12 Quilts from 6 Patterns
© 2002 by Terri Nussbaum

Martingale & Company
20205 144th Avenue NE
Woodinville, WA 98072-8478 USA
www.martingale-pub.com

CREDITS

President . . . . Nancy J. Martin
CEO . . . . Daniel J. Martin
Publisher . . . . Jane Hamada
Editorial Director . . . . Mary V. Green
Managing Editor . . . . Tina Cook
Technical Editor . . . . Laurie Baker
Copy Editor . . . . Ellen Balstad
Design Director . . . . Stan Green
Illustrator . . . . Laurel Strand
Text Designer . . . . Jennifer LaRock Shontz
Cover Designer . . . . Stan Green
Photographer . . . . Brent Kane

Mission Statement

*We are dedicated to providing quality products
and service by working together to inspire
creativity and to enrich the lives we touch.*

Printed in Hong Kong
07 06 05 04 03 02   8 7 6 5 4 3 2 1

DEDICATION

To Kathy Funkhouser. I think of you every time I sit down to sew. Kathy, you gave me a gift I could never repay. It is said that when we practice giving to others we gain the unexpected blessing of receiving extra joy. I am sure that your life is full of joy. May God bless you always.

ACKNOWLEDGMENTS

Life has truly blessed me; first with great parents and a loving family, and then a wonderful husband and a remarkable son. Thank you all for your patience and love.

To the many friends who helped with this book, you were a godsend, and I appreciate all of the work, time, and love you gave me. Thank you to Donna Lever, Kathy Metelica, and Karen Arnzen for your encouragement and support; and to Deb Belcourt, Christy Culver, LuAnn Delong, Jeanne-K Hughs, and Barby Fortin for piecing the samples, and binding and labeling the quilts.

Thank you to Timeless Treasures for supplying the beautiful batik fabric used in "Over the River and through the Trees."

A huge thank you to Jeanine Whittington of Custom Quilts and Design for adding spark to the quilts with her wonderful quilting. It is said that a quilt is not a quilt until it is quilted, and without Jeanine, I am not sure that I would have any quilts at all. Jeanine, I appreciate the fact that you did not close the door on me as I knocked and asked, "Could you quilt this by tomorrow?" You know how untimely I am and you still put up with me; you smiled as you said, "You want it by when?!" Also thanks to Sue Irwin of Tiger Lily Quilting for quilting that one last quilt for me. You and Jeanine are true friends and I am fortunate to have you in my life.

Thanks to Diane Tatterson for her computer skills. The fact that you kept me from putting my fist through the computer screen (or monitor as I guess it is called) was an amazing feat.

Lastly, I would have to say thank you to all of my students who have kept quilting alive and new to me. Your excitement about quilting has kept me going and I have indeed learned much from you. You are fun, and though you start out as students, I am glad you end up as friends.

Library of Congress Cataloging-in-Publication Data
Nussbaum, Terri.
  Quick-change quilts : 12 quilts from 6 patterns /
Terri Nussbaum.
    p. cm.
    ISBN 1-56477-431-7
1. Patchwork—Patterns. 2. Quilting—Patterns. I. Title.
TT835 .N87 2002
746.46'041—dc21
                                                                2002007828

CONTENTS

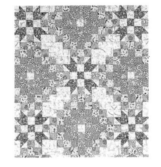

INTRODUCTION

I have been teaching quilting for twenty years, and I am constantly amazed at how many quilters want to make a quilt exactly like the one they've seen on display at the quilt shop or photographed in a book or magazine. One of the wonderful things about being a quilter is the creative aspect, yet many quilters are intimidated by choosing colors or rearranging the blocks in a setting. They want to make exactly what they've seen because they know they like it. While there is nothing wrong with this approach, it is limiting. My hope is that this book will show you how quick and easy it is to take a design and change one or more of the elements to bring out your own personality rather than duplicate what someone else has created.

To get the creative juices flowing, begin by reading "Making Quick Changes" on page 5. This section warms you up with a few simple exercises for making color and design changes to a basic quilt block. From there you'll move on to the big picture and see how block settings and arrangements can give a quilt a completely different look.

At this point you'll no doubt be ready to dive in and start designing your own masterpieces, so I've included some basic information in "General Instructions" on page 7. There you'll find information on selecting and caring for fabric, machine piecing, and the techniques used to make the quilt projects. More information for personalizing and changing your quilts with borders, backing, and labels can be found in "Finishing Touches" on page 13.

Finally, you'll find instructions for six pairs of quilts. Each pair is an example of how one or more of the simple changes discussed in "Making Quick Changes" can create two totally different quilts. Study the quilts and how they differ. But remember, what you see is what worked for me or another quilter. I want you to use the projects as a jumping-off point to create your own versions of those shown. Change the colors, the number of blocks, the way the blocks are arranged, the border treatment, or anything else you can think of to make the quilt fit *your* personality. Have fun!

MAKING QUICK CHANGES

Several years ago an art form called Magic Eye was introduced. To experience the "magic," viewers would focus on a picture, then let their eyes go out of focus. Amazingly, the picture would appear to be something entirely different than what it was when looked at straight on. By letting our eyes blur the obvious, something new and unexpected appears. The same concept can be applied to quilt designs. After you finish a quilt, pin it up on a wall so you can stand back and look at it. From a distance, just stare at it for a while. Now let your eyes go out of focus and see if the colors blur together or the lines of the quilt change. Does this give you any ideas? Can you see different colors in place of the ones you have chosen? Can you see a design change? How far beyond the lines can you see?

CHANGING BLOCKS

Now try a little exercise. Let's say the quilt you were looking at is made up of Star blocks with nine-patch units for centers. The color value of the star points in each block is dark, the center of each Star block—the nine-patch unit—is made up of light and medium values. The star points "pop" because the value of the star points is dark.

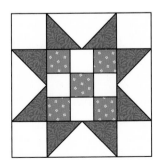

Next, change the value of the star points to medium and use light and dark values for the nine-patch unit. What happened? Is the focus on the nine-patch unit or the star points?

Now let's try a structural change. Remove the nine-patch unit and replace it with a square-in-a-square unit. How has the block changed? Has the focus changed?

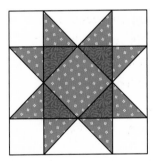

There are many simple changes you can make within a block. Keep playing and see what you can come up with. Let your imagination take you beyond the lines.

CHANGING QUILT SETTINGS

The manner in which you choose to lay out your quilt blocks is called the quilt setting. The quilt setting offers you another opportunity for changes.

There are two basic settings to choose from—straight and diagonal (also referred to as on-point). In straight settings, blocks are laid out in horizontal rows. Diagonal settings are constructed in diagonal rows, using setting triangles to fill in spaces at the edges and corners (refer to "Formulas for Setting Triangles" on page 12).

Straight Setting

Diagonal (On-Point) Setting

The changes you can make within these two settings are endless. Let's take the examples above and make some alterations. Start by adding a simple sashing strip between each block and row. This is a good solution if the pieced blocks are very busy. You can also alternate the main block with a plain block to break up the busyness. Create yet another setting by using pieced sashing.

Straight Setting with Simple Sashing

Diagonal Setting with Plain Blocks

Diagonal Setting with Pieced Sashing

Don't forget that you can also change the arrangement of the blocks within the setting. Look at "The Legal System" on page 58. Rotating the blocks created a lightning-streak design. By setting the light half of all the blocks on the right, another design will appear. Are you beginning to see how many alternatives you have?

GENERAL INSTRUCTIONS

This section will review the basic tools and techniques required for piecing and quilting the projects. If you feel more comfortable using a different tool or assembling the pieces another way, by all means do whatever it takes to make the process enjoyable for you.

FABRIC

Quilters today are fortunate to have such a wide variety of 100 percent–cotton fabrics available to them. You'd be hard-pressed not to find the color or print you were looking for with so many choices. In this section, you'll find information on choosing quality fabrics and how to care for them.

FABRIC QUALITY

Not all fabrics are created equal, and it is important to select a fabric based on its quality as much as its color or print. Why? High-quality fabrics are less likely to shrink, lose dye, and distort during the cutting and piecing processes; this in turn will help you create a quilt you'll be happy with and that will last a long time.

Thread count is a key factor when determining the quality of fabric. Have you ever seen a print at your local quilt shop that is selling for $8.95 per yard, then gone to your local discount retailer and seen the same print for $4.95 a yard? The price difference probably isn't because the discount retailer can buy in bulk and offer the consumer a reduced price. It's more likely that the same design was printed on different greige goods, or base fabric. Fabric manufacturers make several grades of greige goods. The grade of the greige good is dependent on the thread count per square inch. The higher the thread count, the better the fabric. You may have experienced the difference in thread count when purchasing bed sheets. Just compare a 180-thread-count-per-inch sheet with a 220-thread-count sheet, or a 220-thread-count sheet with a 275-thread-count sheet; you'll see what I mean.

The thread count of high-quality quilting cotton should be in the high 60s per square inch, but because the thread count is not listed on fabric as it is on sheets, you'll need to rely on other factors to determine fabric quality. Start with the retailer. Do they purchase only first-run greige goods, which are the highest quality of base fabric available? Feel the fabric. Just as with sheets, a softer fabric usually indicates a higher thread count. However, most fabrics are finished with sizing, which gives them a temporary crispness that will wash out, so be sure to take that into consideration. If any powdery dust appears when you rub the fabric between your fingers, too much sizing has been applied, a device for concealing poor-quality goods. Look at the fabric. Is the print on-grain or off-grain? Are the motifs filled in properly or are they off-register? Scratch the surface of the fabric. Do the threads shift or are they nice and firm? Hold the fabric up to the light and check for any unusually thick or thin areas. These are all signs of fabric quality that you can assess while you're in the store. Fabric shrinkage and dye loss, which you will also need to know about, can only be determined after purchasing.

FABRIC CARE

It's up to you whether to prewash your fabrics. I choose not to prewash my fabrics because I believe the fabric is easier to cut and sew while it still has the sizing on it. I also prefer the antique look my quilts take on because of the small amount of shrinkage that occurs when the quilts are washed and dried the first time. I wash my quilts separately in a large-load washing machine using cold water and Orvus paste. Orvus paste is a mild-formula soap that was originally used to wash livestock. It contains no phosphates and is biodegradable. You can find it in most quilt shops or at farm supply stores.

If you prefer to wash your fabrics before using them, wash light and dark colors separately. After drying the fabrics, iron them, using spray starch or sizing to make them easier to work with.

MACHINE PIECING

When piecing quilts, it is necessary to maintain a consistent ¼"-wide seam allowance. Varying from the ¼" seam allowance will result in blocks that do not finish to the size indicated in the instructions. An incorrect seam allowance can also affect other parts of the quilt, such as sashings and borders.

There are several ways to achieve an accurate ¼" seam allowance. First, many machines have an adjustable needle position that can be set to stitch ¼" from the needle to the outside edge of the presser foot. For some machines, a special quilting foot is available that measures exactly ¼" from the center needle position to the edge of the foot. If your machine does not have either of these options, create a seam guide by placing the edge of a piece of masking tape, moleskin, or a magnetic seam guide exactly ¼" to the right of the needle. The easiest way to do this is to place a clear acrylic ruler under the needle of your machine; then bring the needle down on the first ¼" mark of the ruler. Place the tape, moleskin, or seam guide next to the edge of the ruler.

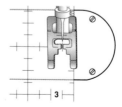 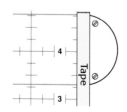

STRIP SETS

You can assemble blocks or parts of blocks that are made up of squares and rectangles by cutting strips of fabric, sewing them together in a particular order to make a strip set, then cutting the strip set into segments. Cut strips for strip sets on the crosswise grain.

The following steps describe the process for making a strip set.

1. Cut and sew the required number and color of strips together as directed in the project instructions. Press the seam allowances toward the darker fabric or as indicated in the project instructions.

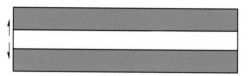

Tip *If you are stitching more than two strips together, alternate the stitching direction with each strip. To prevent distortion, press the seam after each strip is added.*

2. Straighten one end of the strip set. To do this, align a horizontal line of a ruler with an internal seam line of the strip set, placing the ruler at the right-hand edge of the strip set as shown. Cut along the right edge of the ruler.

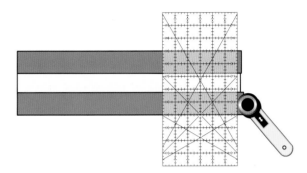

3. Turn the strip set so the straightened edge is on the left-hand side of the mat. From the straightened end, cut segments the width required for your project.

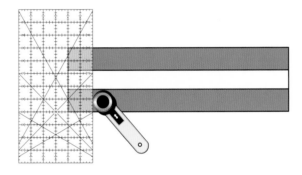

4. Join the segments to make the block units required for your project. Follow pressing directions provided in the project instructions.

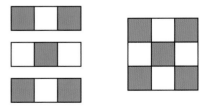

FLIP-AND-SEW CORNERS

This is a clever method for adding corner triangles to a square or rectangle. You may recognize the technique as Mary Ellen Hopkins's connector-square method. It would be more accurate to call these corners "sew-and-flip corners" because you sew through the corner piece first and then flip it up, but I like the sound of "flip-and-sew" better.

The following steps describe how to do a flip-and-sew corner.

1. Using a sharp pencil, draw a diagonal line from corner to corner on the wrong side of the square indicated in the project cutting instructions.

2. With right sides together, place the marked square on the corner of the piece it is to be sewn to, aligning the raw edges. Make sure the diagonal line is positioned in the direction indicated in the project illustration.

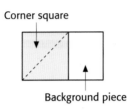

Corner square

Background piece

3. Stitch directly on the diagonal line. Trim the fabric square ¼" from the seam line. Do not trim the corner of the piece it is attached to. Press the resulting triangle toward the corner.

Trim outer corner
of square only.

HALF-SQUARE-TRIANGLE UNITS

A half-square-triangle unit looks like two triangles that have been stitched together to form a square. You can, of course, make a half-square-triangle unit this way, but I prefer the following method. It's not only quick but it also prevents the triangle bias edges from stretching. You will be working with two squares of the same size, usually a light square and a dark square. The squares are stitched together and then cut apart to yield two half-square-triangle units.

The following steps describe the method for making half-square-triangle units.

1. Cut the squares for the half-square-triangle units as directed in the cutting instructions for the project.

2. Using a sharp pencil, draw a diagonal line from corner to corner on the wrong side of the squares indicated in the project instructions. Draw a dashed line ¼" from both sides of the marked line as shown. Be careful not to stretch the fabric as you mark the lines.

3. With right sides together, lay each marked square on top of the remaining color square indicated in the project instructions. Stitch on the dashed lines. Cut the squares apart on the solid line. Press the seams toward the darker fabric unless otherwise noted.

Sew.   Cut.   Press.

ASSEMBLING THE QUILT TOP

Whether you set your blocks in a straight setting or diagonal setting, the blocks are first assembled into rows and then the rows are stitched together. To assemble a straight setting, you arrange your blocks in horizontal rows.

Straight Setting

To assemble a diagonal setting, you arrange your blocks in diagonal rows.

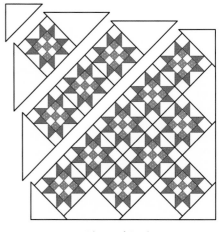

Diagonal Setting

You can see that diagonal settings also differ in that they require setting triangles around the sides and at the corners. Because the setting triangles are cut larger than necessary, you will need to align the square corners of the side setting triangles to the blocks, leaving the excess at the point end of the outside edge of the side setting triangle. Stitch and press the seam; then trim the excess even with the edge of the block.

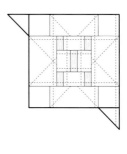

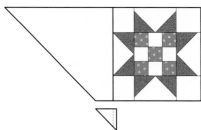

Attach the corner setting triangles last, centering the triangles on the blocks so that any excess or short-fall is distributed equally on each side. When sewn, your quilt top will require some trimming to even out the edges and square up the quilt top.

At this point, decide whether you want to trim the blocks so that only a ¼" seam allowance remains, or leave more than the standard seam allowance so that the blocks appear to float. Whichever you prefer, align your cutting guide with the outside corners of the blocks and then trim as desired, making sure the corners are square and at a 90° angle.

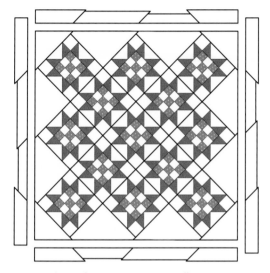

Trimmed to Leave ¼" Seam Allowance

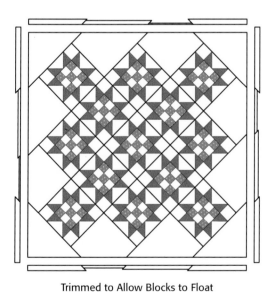

Trimmed to Allow Blocks to Float

PRESSING

Press each seam after it is stitched and before you attach any other pieces to the stitched unit. Begin by pressing the seam flat from the wrong side to smooth out any puckers. Be sure to use the up and down motion of pressing, rather than the gliding motion of ironing, so you do not stretch the fabric. Then open the sewn pieces and, working from the right side, press the seam toward the darker fabric unless otherwise indicated. Use the iron to gently push the fabric over the seam.

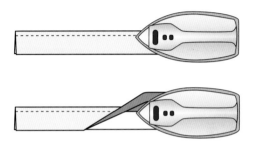

Occasionally, you will be instructed to press the seams open. In these instances, work from the wrong side of the fabric and press very carefully to avoid creases in the seam allowance.

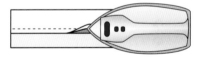

Pressing arrows are included in the project illustrations. Press the seams in the direction indicated to ensure smooth construction of blocks and quilt tops.

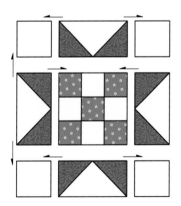

Diagonal or on-point settings require the addition of setting triangles on the quilt sides and at the corners. The following are my formulas for calculating the sizes of the squares needed and instructions for cutting the squares into triangles. These formulas will yield triangles slightly larger than needed. I prefer to make them larger and cut away any excess.

To determine the number of squares to cut for the side setting triangles, count the number of side triangles you will need and divide by 4. Round up to the nearest whole number. Determine the size of square to cut by multiplying the finished block size by 1.41. Add 2½" to this measurement. For example, if your finished block size is 7½", you would cut 13" squares (7.5" x 1.41 + 2.5" = 13.075").

If sashing strips have been added to the block, such as in "Autumn Splendor" on page 18, you will need to add the width of the finished strip to your finished block size and then proceed with the calculation.

Cut each square in half twice diagonally to yield four side setting triangles from each square.

To determine the size to cut squares for the corner triangles, add 1½" to the finished block size. If sashing strips have been stitched to the sides of the blocks, add the finished width of these strips to the finished block size; then add 1½". For example, the blocks in "Autumn Splendor" finish to 8", but a 1½" finished sashing strip has been stitched to each side of the blocks, making the width across the corner 11". You would need to cut 12½" squares for your corner triangles.

Cut two squares to the determined measurement. Cut each square in half once diagonally to yield two corner triangles from each square.

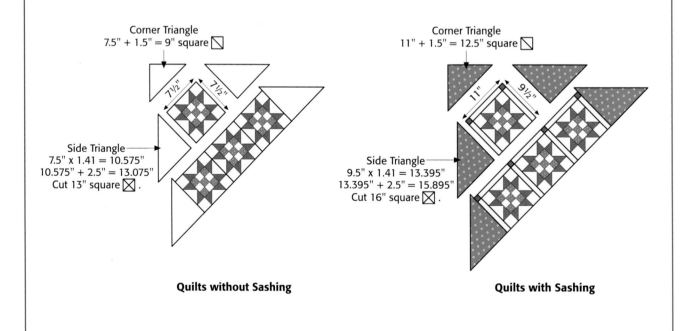

Quilts without Sashing

Corner Triangle
7.5" + 1.5" = 9" square ◻

7½"   7½"

Side Triangle
7.5" x 1.41 = 10.575"
10.575" + 2.5" = 13.075"
Cut 13" square ⊠ .

Quilts with Sashing

Corner Triangle
11" + 1.5" = 12.5" square ◻

11"   9½"

Side Triangle
9.5" x 1.41 = 13.395"
13.395" + 2.5" = 15.895"
Cut 16" square ⊠ .

FINISHING TOUCHES

ADDING BORDERS

Borders should enhance a quilt, much like a frame does a picture. They can add zip and bring the quilt top together, but your eye should focus on the quilt and not be immediately drawn to the borders. In fact, not every quilt needs borders. Often the binding can provide enough of a frame to complement the quilt top. Take for instance "Flying South" (page 26) and "Over the River and through the Trees" (page 27). For "Flying South" I found that the quilt looked finished without any borders, yet for "Over the River and through the Trees," which is a variation of "Flying South," three borders of different widths were used to complement the fabrics and design. And just because you do or don't see a border attached to the quilts in this book doesn't mean you have to replicate them exactly. The fabrics you use may require a different treatment. Remember, it's OK to make changes.

So, how do you decide if your quilt needs borders? It is difficult for even the most experienced quilter to envision what the finished quilt top will look like, so the best thing to do is wait until your quilt top is assembled and then decide if it needs borders. If the quilt doesn't look finished, it probably needs them. Audition different fabrics by placing them next to the quilt top. From there, decide what width is best. This process will ensure that the borders are doing their job, which is to enhance the quilt top.

Because I don't decide on borders until the quilt top is finished, I don't purchase fabric for the borders when I purchase fabrics for the quilt top. If you're afraid that a fabric you think may be an ideal candidate for the border won't be available when you're ready, go ahead and buy it. Just be sure to keep an open mind and go through the auditioning process. The worst thing that can happen if you buy the fabric and it isn't right for the border is that you will end up with a great piece for your stash.

The most important thing to remember about borders is that they must be cut to fit the center measurements of the quilt top. This will ensure the top will have 90° corners and opposite sides will be equal to each other. In the project cutting directions, you will be instructed to cut the strips for borders across the width of the fabric to the width indicated. If your quilt top is longer or wider than 42", stitch the required number of strips together end to end, using a straight or diagonal seam, and recut them to fit the quilt-top edges. Refer to the following instructions to cut the strips to the required lengths and stitch them to the quilt top.

1. Place your quilt top on a flat surface large enough so that you can smooth the top out. Lay 2 border strips across the horizontal center of the quilt top. Trim the strip ends even with the quilt-top raw edges. Fold the border strips in quarters and mark the positions by lightly pressing. Quarter-mark the quilt-top edges and mark the positions with straight pins.

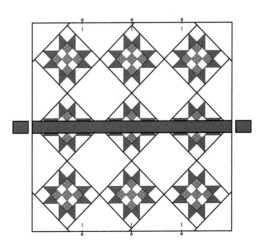

2. With right sides together and raw edges, ends, and quarter-marks matching, sew the borders to the top and bottom edges of the quilt top, easing as necessary. Press the seams toward the borders.

3. Repeat this procedure for the length of the quilt top, laying the border strips across the vertical center of the quilt top.

4. Repeat steps 1–3 to stitch any additional borders to the quilt top.

BACKING AND BATTING

Most of the quilts in this book are wider and longer than 40" and will require that fabric be stitched together to make a piece large enough for the backing. The backing should be cut 6" to 8" larger than the size of the quilt top. I determine how to piece the backing and the yardage needed once I know the quilt size.

For quilts that measure no more than 75" in length or width, I piece the backing with one seam across the width of the quilt. Measure the width of the quilt and add 6" to 8". Double this measurement and divide by 36 to calculate the number of yards of backing fabric you will need.

For quilts that are longer than 75" but no wider than 72", I piece the backing with one lengthwise seam in the center. Measure the length of the quilt and add 6" to 8". Double this measurement and divide by 36 to calculate the number of yards of backing fabric you will need.

Quilts wider than 80" aren't normally wide enough to require more than three lengths of fabric pieced together across the width. Measure the shortest side of the quilt, add 6" to 8", and triple this measurement; divide by 36 to calculate the yardage.

To assemble the backing pieces, remove the selvage edges from the fabric. Cut the fabric into the required number of lengths and stitch them together. Press the seams open.

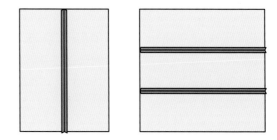

Another possibility for your backing is to use left-over fabrics and/or blocks. Not only are patchwork backings fun and eye-catching, but they also save you from having to purchase the large amount of fabric generally needed for a backing (see photo below). Before making this decision, however, you will need to decide if the quilt will be hand or machine quilted. If you prefer to hand quilt, the extra seams may be a problem; machine quilting may be better.

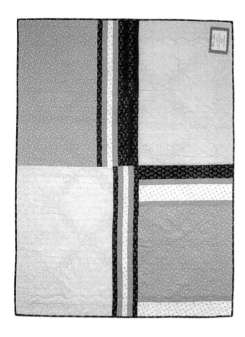

Unfold your batting the day before you plan to baste the quilt. This will allow the batting to relax and expand from having been compressed in the package. Once it has relaxed, cut it the same size as the backing.

ASSEMBLING THE LAYERS

I find the layering and basting process is easier and less stressful for my back if I work on a waist-high tabletop. I use several banquet tables pushed together. Sometimes quilt shops will let you use their classroom tables if they are not using them for classes. A Ping-Pong table or dining-room table are other options, but you will need to protect the surface of the table from the pins. When I used my dining room table, I placed a 4' x 6' piece of plywood on the table before assembling the layers. It was easy to remove and store in the garage until the next quilt was ready to be basted.

To assemble the layers:

1. Press the quilt top and backing to remove any wrinkles or fold lines.
2. Mark the centers of the side edges of the work surface with masking tape. Center the backing on the table, wrong side up. Secure the edges with binder clips or masking tape.
3. Center the batting over the backing. Smooth out any wrinkles, working from the center to the outside edges.
4. Place the quilt top on the batting, centering it and making sure there is about 3" of extra batting and backing on each side. Smooth out any wrinkles, working from the center to the outside edges. Be careful not to stretch the quilt top, and keep any borders and sashing as straight as possible.
5. Baste the layers together, using size 1 rustproof safety pins. Place the pins 4" apart, working from the center out and avoiding any marked quilting lines.

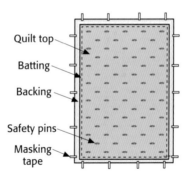

QUILTING

The projects in this book will instruct you to quilt your project "as desired." I prefer to machine quilt, but you may prefer to hand quilt or even tie the layers together to secure them. You may see an opportunity to feature an elaborate design in a plain block, or you may choose to simply stitch in the ditch so a particular fabric takes the spotlight. This is your quilt and quilting presents one more way in which you can personalize it to your own tastes.

BINDING

I cut 2½"-wide strips across the width of the fabric for binding. To calculate the number of strips needed, measure the perimeter of the quilt and add 10". Divide this number by 42 and round up to the nearest whole number. To apply the binding, follow these steps.

1. Sew the strips together to make one long strip; press seams open.

2. Press the strip in half lengthwise, wrong sides together.

3. Trim the excess backing and batting even with the quilt-top edges. With the binding and quilt-top raw edges aligned, place one end of the binding at the center point of one side or at least 15" to 20" from a corner. Leaving a 10" tail and using a ¼" seam allowance, stitch the binding to the quilt. End the stitching ¼" from the corner; backstitch.

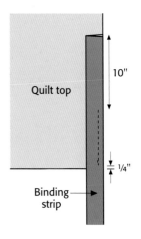

4. To miter the corner, fold the binding strip at a 45° angle away from the quilt. Then fold the binding strip back on itself, parallel with the next edge of the quilt.

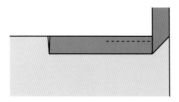

5. Stitch, beginning ¼" from the edge of the fabric. End stitching ¼" from the next corner; backstitch.

6. Repeat steps 4 and 5 for each corner. End stitching 10" from the point where you began stitching, leaving a 6" tail at the end of the binding strip.

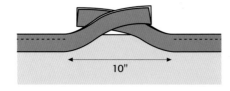

7. Fold the unstitched binding edges back on themselves so they just meet in the middle over the unsewn area of the quilt top. Press the fold.

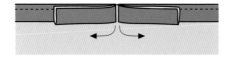

8. Unfold both sides of the binding and match the centers of the pressed Xs. The beginning tail should be on top of the ending tail. Draw a diagonal line from the upper left corner to the lower right through the center of the X. Pin the strips together and stitch on the marked line.

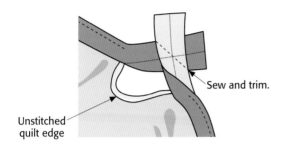

Unstitched quilt edge

Sew and trim.

9. Trim ¼" from the stitched line and press the seam open. Refold the binding, pressing the fold, and stitch the remainder of the binding.

10. Fold the binding from the front of the quilt to the back. The folded edge of the binding should cover the stitching line on the back. Blindstitch the folded edge to the back of the quilt. Stitch the miter that forms at each corner.

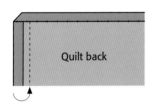

Quilt back

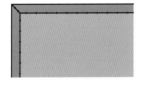

ADDING A LABEL

If you're not already in the practice of stitching a label to the back of your quilts, it would be a good idea to start. Years from now, your family and friends will want to know who made the quilt and when. The label should include at least your name, your city, and the year the quilt was made. I like to name my quilts and add this to the label, as well as the name of the block. If it was quilted by someone other than myself, I include her or his name, too.

AUTUMN SPLENDOR

Project instructions begin on page 20.

By Deb Belcourt, 53½" x 67". Quilted by Sue Irwin.

The blocks are the same, the settings are the same, and both designs separate the blocks with sashing, but these two quilts are different. Simplicity is the key to "Autumn Splendor," which uses just four fabrics for all of the quilt-top elements. Using the same fabric for the simple sashing strips and the block backgrounds makes the blocks appear to float, while the

MARCH WINDS

Project instructions begin on page 22.

By Terri Nussbaum, 70" x 87½"

sashing corner posts flit between them. In contrast, "March Winds" puts a new spin on the blocks by incorporating many fabrics into the larger portion of the pinwheel with string-piecing techniques. The blocks appear as individual components when separated by a three-strip sashing unit with uneven nine-patch units for the corner posts.

Autumn Splendor

Finished Block Size: 8"
Number of Blocks: 18
Setting: Diagonal

MATERIALS

Yardage is based on 42"-wide fabric.

1¾ yds. gold print for blocks, sashing, and inner border

⅝ yd. green print for blocks and sashing corner posts

1¾ yds. blue print for blocks and outer border

2⅛ yds. burgundy print for sashing corner posts, setting triangles, and binding

3¾ yds. fabric for backing

61" x 75" piece of batting

CUTTING

From the gold print, cut:

3 strips, 5¼" x 42"; crosscut the strips into 18 squares, 5¼" x 5¼". Cut each square twice diagonally to yield 72 quarter-square triangles for blocks.

3 strips, 8½" x 42"; crosscut the strips into 48 strips, 2" x 8½", for sashing

6 strips, 2" x 42", for inner border

From the green print, cut:

3 strips, 5¼" x 42"; crosscut the strips into 18 squares, 5¼" x 5¼". Cut each square twice diagonally to yield 72 quarter-square triangles for blocks.

1 strip, 2" x 42"; crosscut the strip into 14 squares, 2" x 2", for sashing corner posts

From the blue print, cut:

5 strips, 4⅞" x 42"; crosscut the strips into 36 squares, 4⅞" x 4⅞". Cut each square once diagonally to yield 72 half-square triangles for blocks.

7 strips, 4½" x 42", for outer border

From the burgundy print, cut:

1 strip, 2" x 42"; crosscut the strips into 17 squares, 2" x 2", for sashing corner posts

2 strips, 16" x 42"; crosscut the strips into 3 squares, 16" x 16". Cut each square twice diagonally to yield 12 side setting triangles (you will use 10 and have 2 left over).

1 strip, 12½" x 42"; crosscut the strip into 2 squares, 12½" x 12½". Cut each square once diagonally to yield 4 corner setting triangles.

8 strips, 2½" x 42", for binding

QUILT-TOP ASSEMBLY

1. Stitch each gold quarter-square triangle to a green quarter-square triangle, placing the straight-grain edge of each triangle as shown. Press the seams toward the green triangles. Make 72 pieced triangles.

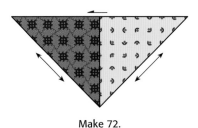

Make 72.

2. Stitch a blue half-square triangle to each pieced triangle. Press the seams toward the blue triangles. Make 72 pieced squares.

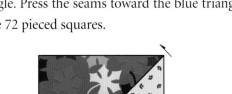

Make 72.

3. Stitch 4 pieced squares together as shown. Press the seams in the directions indicated. Make 18 Double Pinwheel blocks.

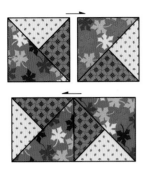 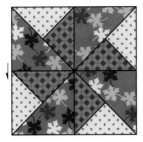

Make 18.

4. Referring to "Assembling the Quilt Top" on page 10, stitch the sashing strips and green and burgundy sashing corner posts into rows as shown. Stitch the blocks and sashing strips into rows as shown. Stitch the sashing rows, block rows, and side setting triangles together using a diagonal setting. Add the corner setting triangles. Trim the edges of the quilt top so they are straight.

QUILT FINISHING

Refer to "Finishing Touches" on pages 13–17.

1. Stitch the inner border and then the outer border to the quilt-top edges.
2. Layer the quilt top with batting and backing; baste.
3. Quilt as desired.
4. Bind the edges and add a label to the quilt back.

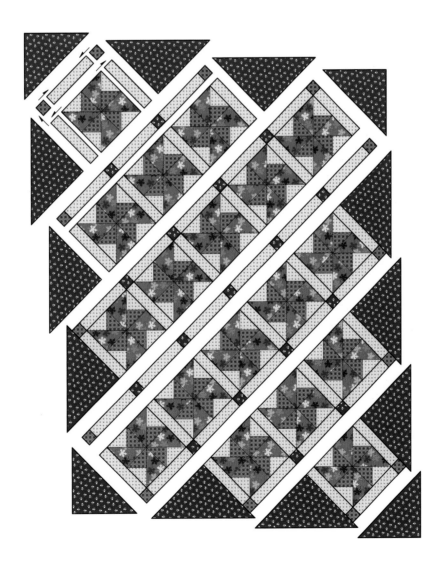

March Winds

Finished Block Size: 8"
Number of Blocks: 18
Setting: Diagonal

MATERIALS

Yardage is based on 42"-wide fabric.

Scraps of assorted-color fabrics for blocks

1⅛ yds. muslin for foundation piecing

3¼ yds. light print for blocks, sashing units, and setting triangles

1⅛ yds. red print for blocks, sashing corner posts, and inner border

1⅜ yds. black print #1 for sashing units

2 yds. black print #2 for outer border and binding

6 yds. fabric for backing

78" x 95" piece of batting

Tip The string-pieced triangles in this quilt are made up of various-size strips, making this project great for using up scraps from previous projects.

CUTTING

From the muslin, cut:

6 strips, 5½" x 42"; crosscut the strips into 36 squares, 5½" x 5½", for foundation of string-pieced triangles for blocks

From the light print, cut:

3 strips, 5¼" x 42"; crosscut the strips into 18 squares, 5¼" x 5¼". Cut each square twice diagonally to yield 72 quarter-square triangles for blocks.

13 strips, 2½" x 42", for sashing units and sashing corner posts

2 strips, 19" x 42"; crosscut the strips into 3 squares, 19" x 19". Cut each square twice diagonally to yield 12 side setting triangles (you will use 10 and have 2 left over).

1 strip, 16½" x 42"; crosscut the strip into 2 squares, 16½" x 16½". Cut each square once diagonally to yield 4 corner setting triangles.

From the red print, cut:

3 strips, 5¼" x 42"; crosscut the strips into 18 squares, 5¼" x 5¼". Cut each square twice diagonally to yield 72 quarter-square triangles for blocks.

4 strips, 1¼" x 42", for sashing corner posts

7 strips, 2" x 42", for inner border

From black print #1, cut:

28 strips, 1¼" x 42", for sashing units

2 strips, 2½" x 42", for sashing corner posts

From black print #2, cut:

8 strips, 5" x 42", for outer border

9 strips, 2½" x 42", for binding

QUILT-TOP ASSEMBLY

1. To make string-pieced triangles, cut the assorted-color scraps into strips that are 1" to 3" wide and at least 6" long. Place a strip on the left side of a 6" muslin square, right side up. Holding the first strip in place with your fingers, place the second strip over the first strip, right sides together. Position the second strip so the right-hand edge of the first strip will be covered when the second strip is stitched in place and pressed over to the right side. Stitch the strip in place along the right edge, using a ¼" wide seam allowance. Press the second strip to the right side. Continue adding strips until the entire square is covered. You may place the strips at any angle as long as the right-hand edge of the previous strip will be covered when the next strip is stitched to it. Make 36 string-pieced blocks.

2. Trim each string-pieced block to 4⅞" x 4⅞". Cut each block once diagonally to yield 72 half-square triangles for the blocks. Set the triangles aside.

3. Stitch each red quarter-square triangle to a light print quarter-square triangle, placing the straight-grain edge of each triangle as shown. Press the seams toward the red triangles. Make 72 pieced triangles.

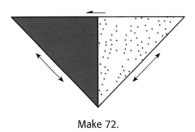

Make 72.

4. Stitch a string-pieced half-square triangle to each pieced triangle. Press the seams toward the pieced triangles. Make 72 pieced squares.

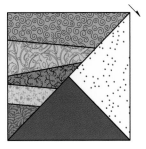

Make 72.

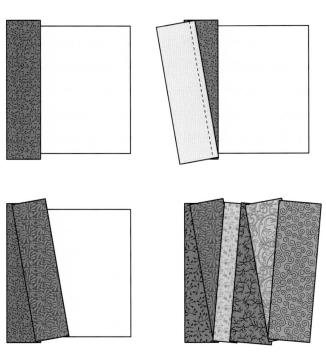

Make 36.

5. Stitch 4 pieced squares together as shown. Press the seams in the direction indicated. Make 18 Double Pinwheel blocks.

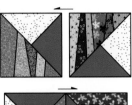

Make 18.

6. Referring to "Strip Sets" on page 8, stitch a 1¼" x 42" black print #1 strip to each side of a light print 2½" x 42" strip. Press the seams toward the black strips. Make 13 strip sets. Crosscut the strip sets into 48 segments, each 8½" wide, for the sashing units, and 31 segments, each 2½" wide, for the sashing corner posts.

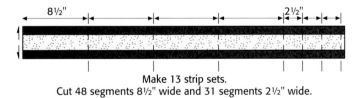

8½"   2½"

Make 13 strip sets.
Cut 48 segments 8½" wide and 31 segments 2½" wide.

7. Stitch a red 1¼" x 42" strip to each side of a 2½" x 42" black print #1 strip. Press the seams toward the black strip. Make 2. Crosscut the strips into 62 segments, each 1¼" wide, for the sashing corner posts.

1¼"

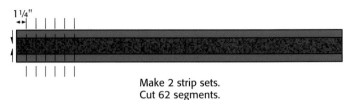

Make 2 strip sets.
Cut 62 segments.

8. To complete the sashing corner posts, stitch a 1¼" wide segment from step 7 to each side of a 2½" wide segment from step 6. Press the seams toward the center strip. Make 31.

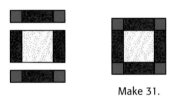

Make 31.

9. Referring to "Assembling the Quilt Top" on page 10, stitch the sashing units and sashing corner posts into rows as shown. Stitch the blocks and sashing units into rows as shown. Stitch the sashing rows, block rows, and side setting triangles together using a diagonal setting. Add the corner setting triangles. Trim the edges of the quilt top so they are straight.

QUILT FINISHING

Refer to "Finishing Touches" on pages 13–17.

1. Stitch the inner border and then the outer border to the quilt-top edges.
2. Layer the quilt top with batting and backing; baste.
3. Quilt as desired.
4. Bind the edges and add a label to the quilt back.

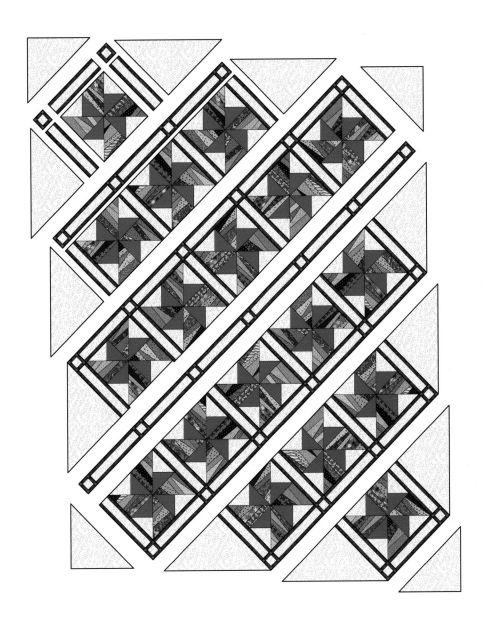

FLYING SOUTH

Project instructions begin on page 28.

By Terri Nussbaum, 64" x 80". Quilted by Jeanine Whittington.

These two quilts use the same units to make up the blocks, but color, block arrangement, and row arrangement make them look totally different. "Flying South" takes a scrappy approach, using an assortment of dark prints for the geese and gold and rust prints for the rails. Each block and each row are arranged identically, leaving all the geese rows heading south as

OVER THE RIVER AND THROUGH THE TREES

Project instructions begin on page 30.

By Christy Culver, 78½" x 94½" Quilted by Jeanine Whittington.

nature intended. "Over the River and through the Trees" features two blocks that are a variation of the one used for "Flying South." Blocks are alternated within the rows to give the illusion that the geese are flying between trees.

Flying South

Finished Block Size: 16"
Number of Blocks: 20
Setting: Straight

MATERIAL

Yardage is based on 42"-wide fabric.

4⅝ yds. *total* of assorted gold prints for flying-geese units and split-rail units

2⅞ yds. *total* of assorted dark prints that measure at least 2½" x 4½" for flying-geese units

1⅝ yds. *total* of assorted rust prints for split-rail units

5¾ yds. fabric for backing

72" x 88" piece of batting

¾ yd. fabric for binding

CUTTING

From the assorted gold prints, cut:

640 squares, 2½" x 2½", for flying-geese units

80 strips, 2½" x 8½", for split-rail units

From the assorted dark prints, cut:

320 rectangles, 2½" x 4½", for flying-geese units

From the assorted rust prints, cut:

80 strips, 2½" x 8½", for split-rail units

From the binding fabric, cut:

8 strips, 2½" x 42"

QUILT-TOP ASSEMBLY

1. To make the flying-geese units, refer to "Flip-and-Sew Corners" on page 9 to mark a diagonal line on the wrong side of each gold print 2½" square. Stitch 1 square to each end of each dark print 2½" x 4½" rectangle. Trim the corner of the squares. Press the seams toward the gold triangles. Make 320 flying-geese units.

Make 320.

2. Stitch 4 flying-geese units together as shown. Press the seams in the direction shown. Make 80 flying-geese strips.

Make 80.

3. To make the split-rail units, stitch each gold print 2½" x 8½" strip to a rust print 2½" x 8½" strip. Press the seams toward the rust strips. Make 80 split-rail units.

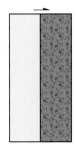

Make 80.

4. With the flying-geese unit points up, stitch a split-rail unit to the left-hand side of the flying-geese strip as shown to make block A. Make 40. Repeat to stitch the remaining split-rail units to the right-hand side of the remaining flying-geese strips to make block B. Make 40. Press the seams toward the split-rail units.

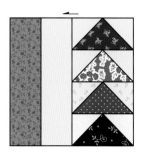 

Block A
Make 40.

Block B
Make 40.

5. Arrange 2 of block A and 2 of block B as shown to make the Geese and Rails block. Make 20.

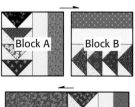 

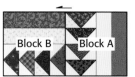

Make 20.

6. Referring to "Assembling the Quilt Top" on page 10, arrange the blocks into 5 horizontal rows of 4 blocks each as shown. Stitch the blocks in each row together. Press the seams in opposite directions from row to row. Stitch the rows together. Press the seams in one direction.

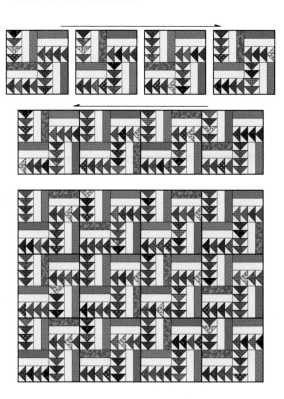

QUILT FINISHING

Refer to "Finishing Touches" on pages 13–17.

1. Layer the quilt top with batting and backing; baste.
2. Quilt as desired.
3. Bind the edges and add a label to the quilt back.

Over the River and through the Trees

Finished Block Size: 16"
Number of Blocks: 20
Setting: Straight

MATERIALS

Yardage is based on 42"-wide fabric.

4⅝ yds. blue print for flying-geese units and split-rail units

2⅞ yds. pink print for flying-geese units and middle border

2¼ yds. green print for flying-geese units

1⅝ yds. yellow print for split-rail units

½ yd. dark blue print for inner border

1⅛ yds. multicolor print for outer border

7⅞ yds. fabric for backing

¾ yd. fabric for binding

86" x 102" piece of batting

CUTTING

From the blue print, cut:

40 strips, 2½" x 42"; crosscut the strips to make 640 squares, 2½" x 2½", for flying-geese units

20 strips, 2½" x 42", for split-rail units

From the pink print, cut:

16 strips, 4½" x 42"; crosscut the strips into 160 rectangles, 2½" x 4½", for flying-geese units

8 strips, 2½" x 42", for middle border

From the green print, cut:

16 strips, 4½" x 42"; crosscut the strips into 160 rectangles, 2½" x 4½", for flying-geese units

From the yellow print, cut:

20 strips, 2½" x 42", for split-rail units

From the dark blue print, cut:

8 strips, 1¾" x 42", for inner border

From the multicolor print, cut:

8 strips, 4½" x 42", for outer border

From the binding fabric, cut:

9 strips, 2½" x 42"

QUILT-TOP ASSEMBLY

1. To make the flying-geese units, refer to "Flip-and-Sew Corners" on page 9 to mark a diagonal line on the wrong side of each blue print 2½" square. Stitch 1 square to each end of each pink print and each green print 2½" x 4½" rectangle. Trim the corner of the squares. Press the seams toward the blue triangles. Make 160 pink and 160 green flying-geese units.

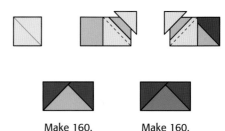

Make 160.   Make 160.

2. Stitch 4 pink flying-geese units together as shown. Press the seams in the direction shown. Make 40 pink flying-geese strips. Repeat to make 40 green flying-geese strips. Press the seam allowances on half of the units in one direction; press the seam allowances on the remaining units in the opposite direction.

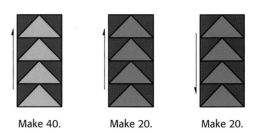

Make 40.   Make 20.   Make 20.

3. To make the split-rail units, refer to "Strip Sets" on page 8 to stitch each blue print 2½" x 42" strip to a yellow print 2½" x 42" strip. Make 20. Press the seams toward the blue strips. Crosscut the strips into 80 split-rail units, each 8½" wide.

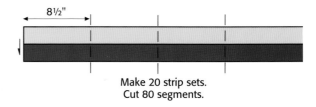

8½"

Make 20 strip sets.
Cut 80 segments.

4. With the flying-geese unit points up, stitch a split-rail unit to the left-hand side of 20 pink and 20 green flying-geese units (seam allowance pressed up) as shown to make block A. Repeat to stitch the remaining split-rail units to the right-hand side of the remaining 20 pink and 20 green flying-geese units (seam allowance pressed down) to make block B. Press the seams toward the split-rail units.

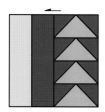 

Block A
Make 20 pink
and 20 green.

Block B
Make 20 pink
and 20 green.

5. Stitch 1 green block A, 2 pink block As, and 1 pink block B together as shown to make the Geese and Rails Variation I block. Make 10. Stitch 1 green block A, 2 green block Bs, and 1 pink block B together as shown to make the Geese and Rails Variation II block. Make 10.

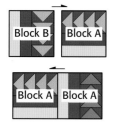

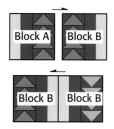

Geese and Rails Variation I
Make 10.

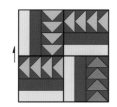

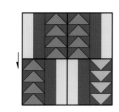

Geese and Rails Variation II
Make 10.

6. Referring to "Assembling the Quilt Top" on page 10, arrange the blocks into 5 horizontal rows of 4 blocks each, alternating the Variation I and Variation II blocks in each row as shown. Stitch the blocks in each row together. Press the seams in opposite directions from row to row. Stitch the rows together. Press the seams in one direction.

QUILT FINISHING

Refer to "Finishing Touches" on pages 13–17.

1. Stitch the inner border, the middle border, and then the outer border to the quilt-top edges.
2. Layer the quilt top with batting and backing; baste.
3. Quilt as desired.
4. Bind the edges and add a label to the quilt back.

OCTOBER SKY

Project instructions begin on page 34.

By Terri Nussbaum, 74¾" x 98½". Quilted by Jeanine Whittington.

Place these quilts side by side and most folks will tell you that there are no similarities between the two. Even though both quilts are made up of Churn Dash and Shoo Fly blocks, and the blocks are arranged in the same setting, the colors give each quilt its own identity. "October Sky" employs just four fabrics for the quilt top, and each fabric is placed in

AMISH SKIES

Project instructions begin on page 38.

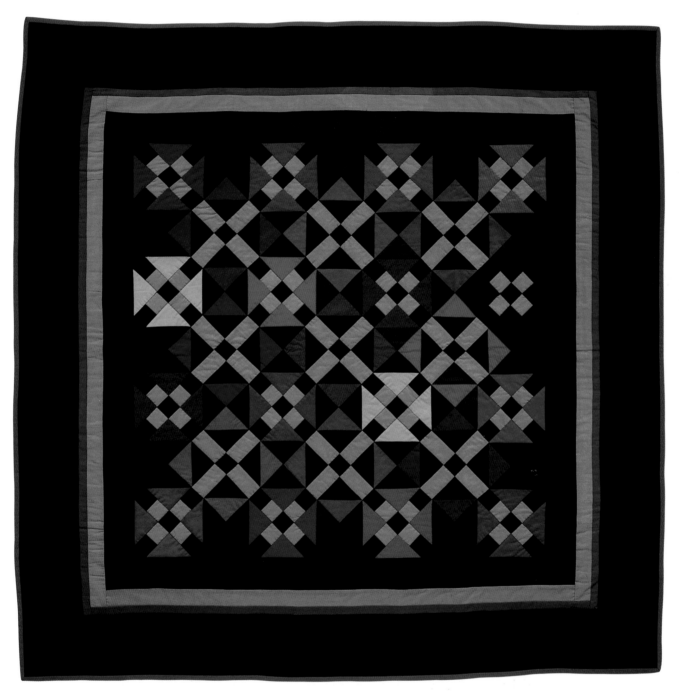

By Terri Nussbaum, 63½" x 63½". Quilted by Sue Smith.

exactly the same position within each block. For "Amish Skies," the dark and gold fabrics in the center portion of each block remain the same, but splashes of randomly selected colors also appear.

October Sky

| Finished Block Size: 7½" |
| Number of Blocks: 59 |
| Setting: Diagonal |

MATERIALS

Yardage is based on 42"-wide fabric.

2⅛ yds. light floral print for blocks

⅞ yd. light pink print for blocks

1⅜ yds. black small-scale print for blocks

2¼ yds. medium gold print for blocks and setting triangles

¾ yd. wine print for inner border

2¼ yds. dark floral print for outer border and binding

6½ yds. fabric for backing

82" x 106" piece of batting

Tip *If you're having trouble choosing the fabrics for this quilt or another, start with a "palette" fabric—a fabric you like that has a variety of colors in it. On the selvage edge of the fabric, most manufacturers place dots of colors that match the fabric. You can use these dots to select additional fabrics that match your palette fabric.*

CUTTING

From the light floral print, cut:

12 strips, 3⅞" x 42"; crosscut the strips into 118 squares, 3⅞" x 3⅞", for Churn Dash and Shoo Fly block half-square-triangle units

9 strips, 2" x 42", for Churn Dash block strip sets

From the light pink print, cut:

5 strips, 3⅞" x 42"; crosscut the strips into 48 squares, 3⅞" x 3⅞", for Churn Dash block half-square-triangle units

2 strips, 2" x 42", for Shoo Fly block strip sets

From the black small-scale print, cut:

7 strips, 3⅞" x 42"; crosscut the strips into 70 squares, 3⅞" x 3⅞", for Shoo Fly block half-square-triangle units

7 strips, 2" x 42", for Churn Dash block strip sets

From the medium gold print, cut:

8 strips, 3½" x 42"; crosscut 4 strips into 70 rectangles, 2" x 3½", for Shoo Fly blocks. Set the remaining 4 strips aside for Shoo Fly block strip sets.

2 strips, 13" x 42"; crosscut the strips into 5 squares, 13" x 13". Cut each square twice diagonally to yield 20 side setting triangles.

2 squares, 9" x 9"; cut each square once diagonally to yield 4 corner setting triangles

From the wine print, cut:

8 strips, 2½" x 42", for inner border

From the dark floral print, cut:

8 strips, 6" x 42", for outer border

9 strips, 2½" x 42", for binding

QUILT-TOP ASSEMBLY

1. Refer to "Half-Square-Triangle Units" on page 9 to make the half-square-triangle units for the blocks. For the Churn Dash blocks, use 48 each of the light floral and light pink 3⅞" squares. For the Shoo Fly blocks, use 70 each of the light floral and black print 3⅞" squares. Press the seams toward the black print and light pink triangles. You should have 96 light-floral-and-light-pink half-square-triangle units and 140 light-floral-and-black-print half-square-triangle units.

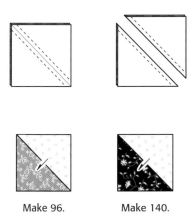

Make 96. Make 140.

2. Refer to "Strip Sets" on page 8 to make the strip sets for the blocks. For the Churn Dash blocks, stitch 3 light floral and 2 black 2" x 42" strips together as shown to make strip set A. Press the seams toward the black strips. Make 2. Crosscut the strip sets into 24 segments, each 2" wide. In the same manner, stitch 1 light floral and 1 black 2" x 42" strip together to make strip set B. Press the seam toward the black strip. Make 3. Crosscut the strip sets into 48 segments, each 2" wide. For the Shoo Fly Blocks, stitch 2 medium gold 3½" x 42" strips to each side of a light pink 2" x 42" strip to make strip set C. Press the seams toward the light pink strip. Make 2. Crosscut the strip sets into 35 segments, each 2".

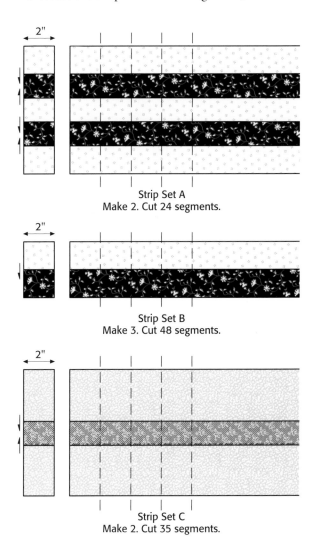

Strip Set A
Make 2. Cut 24 segments.

Strip Set B
Make 3. Cut 48 segments.

Strip Set C
Make 2. Cut 35 segments.

3. To make the Churn Dash blocks, stitch 4 light-floral-and-light-pink half-square-triangle units, 1 strip set A segment, and 2 strip set B segments together as shown. Press the seams in the directions indicated. Make 24.

4. To make the Shoo Fly blocks, stitch 4 light-floral-and-black half-square-triangle units, 1 strip set C segment, and 2 medium gold 2" x 3½" rectangles together as shown. Press the seams in the directions indicated. Make 35.

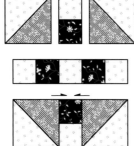

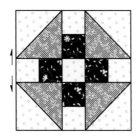

Make 24.

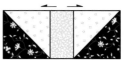

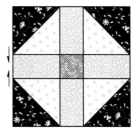

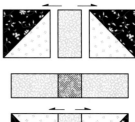

Make 35.

Tip Cut additional 2"-wide segments from your left-over strip sets and combine them with 3½" light floral, light pink, and black print squares to make additional blocks. Combine four blocks to make a pillow to coordinate with your quilt.

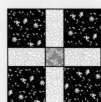

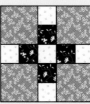

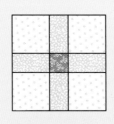

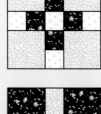

5. Referring to "Assembling the Quilt Top" on page 10, alternately arrange the blocks into 11 diagonal rows as shown. Stitch the blocks in each row together, adding the appropriate side setting triangles at the ends of each row. Press the seams toward the side setting triangles and the Churn Dash blocks. Stitch the rows together. Add the remaining corner setting triangles. Trim the edges of the quilt top so they are straight.

QUILT FINISHING

Refer to "Finishing Touches" on pages 13–17.

1. Stitch the inner border and then the outer border to the quilt-top edges.
2. Layer the quilt top with batting and backing; baste.
3. Quilt as desired.
4. Bind the edges and add a label to the quilt back.

Amish Skies

Finished Block Size: 7½"
Number of Blocks: 25
Setting: Diagonal

MATERIALS

Yardage is based on 42"-wide fabric.

¾ yd. *total* of assorted bright solids for blocks

2 yds. *total* of assorted dark solids for blocks and
setting triangles

1⅛ yds. gold solid for blocks and inner border

⅜ yd. green solid for middle border

1⅛ yds. black solid for outer border

⅝ yd. red solid for binding

4½ yds. fabric for backing

72" x 72" square of batting

CUTTING

From the assorted bright solids, cut a *total* of:

25 matching pairs of squares (50 total), 3⅞" x 3⅞",
for Churn Dash and Shoo Fly block half-square-
triangle units

From the assorted dark solids, cut a *total* of:

50 squares, 3⅞" x 3⅞", for Churn Dash and Shoo Fly
block half-square-triangle units

6 strips, 2" x 42", for Churn Dash and Shoo Fly block
strip sets

3 squares, 13" x 13"; cut each square twice diagonally
to yield 12 side setting triangles

2 squares, 9" x 9"; cut each square once diagonally to
yield 4 corner setting triangles

From the gold solid, cut:

10 strips, 2" x 42", for Churn Dash block strip sets
and inner border

4 strips, 3½" x 42"; crosscut 2 strips into 36 rectangles,
each 2" x 3½", for Shoo Fly blocks. Set the remaining 2 strips aside for Shoo Fly block strip sets.

From the green solid, cut:

6 strips, 1¼" x 42", for middle border

From the black solid, cut:

6 strips, 6" x 42", for outer border

From the red solid, cut:

7 strips, 2½" x 42", for binding

QUILT-TOP ASSEMBLY

1. Stitch each assorted bright 3⅞" square to an
   assorted dark 3⅞" square, referring to "Half-
   Square-Triangle Units" on page 9. Press the seams
   toward the dark triangles. Make 100.

Make 100
total.

2. Refer to "Strip Sets" on page 8 to make the strip sets
   for the blocks. For the Churn Dash blocks, stitch 3
   dark and 2 gold 2" x 42" strips together as shown to
   make strip set A. Press the seams toward the dark
   strips. Make 1. Crosscut the strip set into 16 segments, each 2" wide. In the same manner, stitch 1
   dark and 1 gold 2" x 42" strip together to make strip
   set B. Press the seam toward the dark strip. Make 2.
   Crosscut the strip sets into 32 segments,
   each 2" wide. For the Shoo Fly Blocks,
   stitch 2 gold 3½" x 42" strips to each side of a dark
   2" x 42" strip to make strip set C. Press the seams

toward the gold strips. Make 1. Crosscut the strip set into 9 segments, each 2".

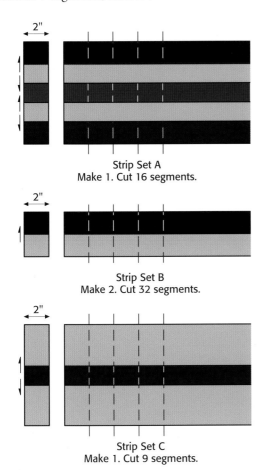

Strip Set A
Make 1. Cut 16 segments.

Strip Set B
Make 2. Cut 32 segments.

Strip Set C
Make 1. Cut 9 segments.

3. To make the Churn Dash blocks, stitch 4 half-square-triangle units with the same bright-color half, 1 strip set A segment, and 2 strip set B segments together as shown. Press the seams in the directions indicated. Make 16.

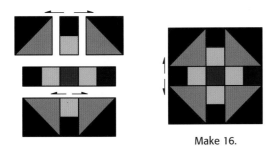

Make 16.

4. To make the Shoo Fly blocks, stitch 4 half-square-triangle units with the same bright-color half, 1 strip set C segment, and 2 gold 2" x 3½" rectangles together as shown. Press the seams in the directions indicated. Make 9.

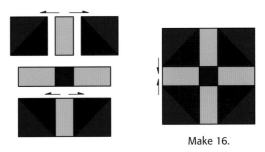

Make 16.

5. Referring to "Assembling the Quilt Top" on page 10, alternately arrange the blocks into 7 diagonal rows as shown. Stitch the blocks in each row together, adding the appropriate side setting triangles at the ends of each row. Press the seams toward the side setting triangles and the Shoo Fly blocks. Stitch the rows together. Add the corner setting triangles. Trim the edges of the quilt top so they are straight.

QUILT FINISHING

Refer to "Finishing Touches" on pages 13–17.

1. Stitch the inner border, then the middle border, and finally the outer border to the quilt-top edges.
2. Layer the quilt top with batting and backing; baste.
3. Quilt as desired.
4. Bind the edges and add a label to the quilt back.

WINTER SOLSTICE

Project instructions begin on page 42.

By Terri Nussbaum, 65½" x 85½". Quilted by Jeanine Whittington.

Look at the incredible change that occurs when a solid block is replaced with a pieced block.
Both quilts feature the star-like Sisters block. In "Winter Solstice," the Sisters blocks form a
chain across the lighter plain blocks; the dark colors recede against the lighter plain blocks.

TRIPPING THROUGH THE STARS

Project instructions begin on page 46.

By Terri Nussbaum, 66½" x 86½". Quilted by Jeanine Whittington.

Now look at "Tripping through the Stars." Here, Many Trips blocks take the place of the plain blocks, and the Sisters blocks suddenly show up in twinkling splendor.

Winter Solstice

Finished Block Size: 7½"
Number of Blocks: 35
Setting: Straight

MATERIALS

Yardage is based on 42"-wide fabric.

1⅛ yds. red print for Sisters blocks and middle border

3 yds. dark blue print for Sisters blocks, sashing units, outer border, and binding

1½ yds. medium blue print for Sisters blocks, sashing units, and inner border

1¾ yds. light floral print for plain blocks and sashing units

6 yds. fabric for backing

74" x 94" piece of batting

Tip When choosing a background fabric, consider the quilting design you'd like for the large spaces. If you want your quilting stitches to show, use a fabric with a design that's not too busy. If you want to hide your quilting, select a busy fabric with lots of patterns.

CUTTING

From the red print, cut:

5 strips, 2⅜" x 42"; crosscut the strips into 72 squares, 2⅜" x 2⅜", for half-square-triangle units

5 strips, 2" x 42", for block strip sets

7 strips, 1½" x 42", for middle border

From the dark blue print, cut:

5 strips, 2⅜" x 42"; crosscut the strips into 72 squares, 2⅜" x 2⅜", for half-square-triangle units

8 strips, 2" x 42"; crosscut 4 strips into 72 squares, each 2" x 2", for block corner squares. Set the remaining 4 strips aside for block strip sets.

3 strips, 3½" x 42"; crosscut the strips into 24 squares, 3½" x 3½", for sashing

7 strips, 5½" x 42", for outer border

8 strips, 2½" x 42", for binding

From the medium blue print, cut:

16 strips, 2" x 42"; crosscut 2 strips into 36 squares, 2" x 2", for blocks. Set the remaining 14 strips aside for block strip sets and sashing strip sets.

7 strips, 2" x 42", for inner border

From the light floral print, cut:

4 strips, 8" x 42"; crosscut the strips into 17 squares, 8" x 8", for plain blocks

3 strips, 2" x 42", for sashing strip sets

3 strips, 5" x 42", for sashing strip sets

QUILT-TOP ASSEMBLY

1. Refer to "Half-Square-Triangle Units" on page 9 to make the half-square-triangle units for the Sisters blocks. Use the red print and dark blue print 2⅜" squares. Press the seams toward the dark blue triangles. Make 144.

Make 144.

2. Refer to "Strip Sets" on page 8 to make the block strip sets and sashing strip sets, using the 2" x 42" strips. For the Sisters blocks, stitch a red print 2" x 42" strip to each side of a dark blue 2" x 42" strip to make strip set A. Press the seams toward the red print strips. Make 2. Cut the strip sets into 36 segments, each 2" wide. To make strip set B, stitch 1 red, 2 medium blue, and 2 dark blue 2" x 42" strips together as shown. Press the seams in the directions indicated. Make 1. Cut the strip set into 18 segments, each 2" wide. For the sashing, stitch 1 light floral, 2 dark blue, and 2 medium blue 2" x 42" strips together as shown to make strip set C. Press the seams in the directions indicated. Make 3. Crosscut the strip sets into 58 segments, each 2" wide. To make strip set D, stitch a medium blue 2" x 42" strip to each side of a light floral 5" x 42" strip. Press the seams in the directions indicated. Make 3. Crosscut the strip sets into 58 segments, each 2" wide.

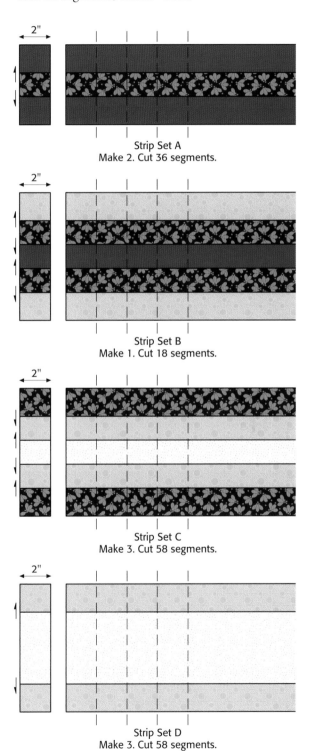

Strip Set A
Make 2. Cut 36 segments.

Strip Set B
Make 1. Cut 18 segments.

Strip Set C
Make 3. Cut 58 segments.

Strip Set D
Make 3. Cut 58 segments.

3. To make the Sisters block, stitch 4 dark blue 2" squares, 2 medium blue 2" squares, 8 red-and-dark-blue half-square-triangle units, 2 strip set A segments, and 1 strip set B segment together into 5 horizontal rows as shown. Press the seams in the directions indicated. Stitch the rows together. Press the seams in the directions indicated. Make 18.

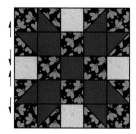

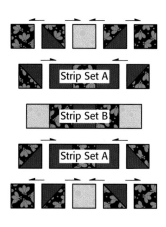

Make 18.

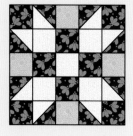

Tip *Replace the red print in this block with a light-colored fabric and the star will come bursting to life.*

4. To make the sashing units, stitch each strip set C segment to a strip set D segment as shown. Press the seams toward the strip set C segments. Make 58 sashing units.

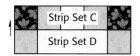

Make 58.

5. To make the block rows, stitch 3 Sisters blocks, 2 plain blocks, and 4 sashing units together as shown. Pay special attention to the orientation of the sashing units. Press the seams toward the sashing units. Make 4 rows. To make the alternating rows, stitch 3 plain blocks, 2 Sisters block, and 4 sashing strips together as shown. Press the seams toward the sashing units. Make 3 rows.

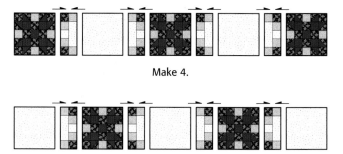

Make 4.

Make 3.

6. To make the sashing rows, stitch 5 sashing units and 4 dark blue 3½" squares together as shown below. Pay special attention to the orientation of the sashing units. Press the seams toward the sashing units. Make 6 rows.

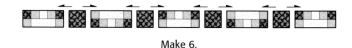

Make 6.

7. Alternately stitch the block rows and sashing rows together as shown on page 45.

QUILT FINISHING

Refer to "Finishing Touches" on pages 13–17.

1. Stitch the inner border, then the middle border, and finally the outer border to the quilt-top edges.

2. Layer the quilt top with batting and backing; baste.

3. Quilt as desired.

4. Bind the edges and add a label to the quilt back.

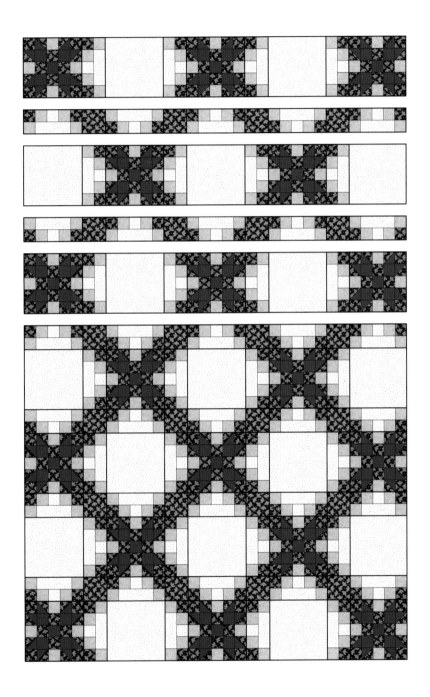

Tripping through the Stars

Finished Block Size: 7½"
Number of Blocks: 35
Setting: Straight

MATERIALS

Yardage is based on 42"-wide fabric.

1⅛ yds. dark pink print for Sisters blocks and inner border

1¾ yds. cream print for Sisters blocks, Many Trips blocks, and sashing units

1⅛ yds. light purple print for Sisters blocks and sashing units

⅝ yd. dark purple print for Many Trips blocks

⅞ yd. yellow print for Many Trips blocks and sashing units

¾ yd. green print #1 for Many Trips blocks and sashing units

⅜ yd. medium pink print for Many Trips blocks

⅝ yd. yellow solid for middle border

1⅛ yds. green print #2 for outer border

¾ yd. blue print for binding

6 yds. fabric for backing

74" x 94" piece of batting

CUTTING

From the dark pink print, cut:

5 strips, 2⅜" x 42"; crosscut the strips into 72 squares, 2⅜" x 2⅜", for half-square-triangle units

5 strips, 2" x 42", for strip sets

7 strips, 2" x 42", for inner border

From the cream print, cut:

5 strips, 2⅜" x 42"; crosscut the strips into 72 squares, 2⅜" x 2⅜", for half-square-triangle units

15 strips, 2" x 42"; crosscut 4 strips into 72 squares, each 2" x 2", for Sisters block corner squares. Set the remaining 11 strips aside for strip sets.

3 strips, each 3½" x 42"; crosscut the strips into 24 squares, 3½" x 3½", for sashing

From the light purple print, cut:

16 strips, 2" x 42"; cut 2 strips into 36 squares, 2" x 2", for Sisters blocks. Set the remaining 14 strips aside for strip sets.

From the dark purple print, cut:

8 strips, 2" x 42", for strip sets

From the yellow print, cut:

13 strips, 2" x 42", for strip sets

From green print #1, cut:

11 strips, 2" x 42", for strip sets

From the medium pink print, cut:

4 strips, 2" x 42", for strip sets

From the yellow solid, cut:

7 strips, 2½" x 42", for middle border

From green print #2, cut:

7 strips, 5" x 42", for outer border

From the blue print, cut:

8 strips, 2½" x 42", for binding

QUILT-TOP ASSEMBLY

1. Refer to "Half-Square-Triangle Units" on page 9 to make the half-square-triangle units for the Sisters blocks, using the dark pink print and cream print 2⅜" squares. Press the seams toward the dark pink triangles. Make 144.

Make 144.

2. Refer to "Strip Sets" on page 8 to make the block strip sets and sashing unit strip sets, using the 2" x 42" strips. For the Sisters blocks, stitch a dark pink strip to each side of a cream strip to make strip set A. Make 2. To make strip set B, stitch 1 dark pink, 2 light purple, and 2 cream strips together as shown. Make 1.

For the Many Trips blocks, stitch 1 dark purple, 2 yellow print, and 2 green print #1 strips together as shown to make strip set C. Make 2. To make strip set D, stitch 1 medium pink, 2 green print #1, and 2 dark purple strips together as shown. Make 2. To make strip set E, stitch 1 cream, 2 dark purple, and 2 medium pink strips together as shown. Make 1.

For the sashing units, stitch 1 green print #1, 2 light purple, and 2 yellow print strips together as shown to make strip set F. Make 3. To make strip set G, stitch 1 yellow print, 2 cream, and 2 light purple strips together as shown. Make 3.

Press all of the seam allowances in the directions indicated. Cut the strip sets into 2"-wide segments as follows: strip set A, 36; strip set B, 18; strip sets C and D, 34 each; strip set E, 17; strip sets F and G, 58 each.

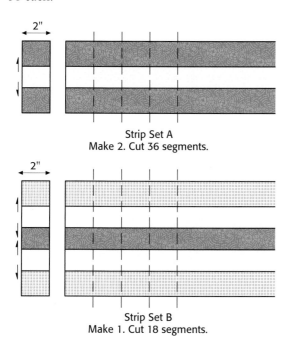

Strip Set A
Make 2. Cut 36 segments.

Strip Set B
Make 1. Cut 18 segments.

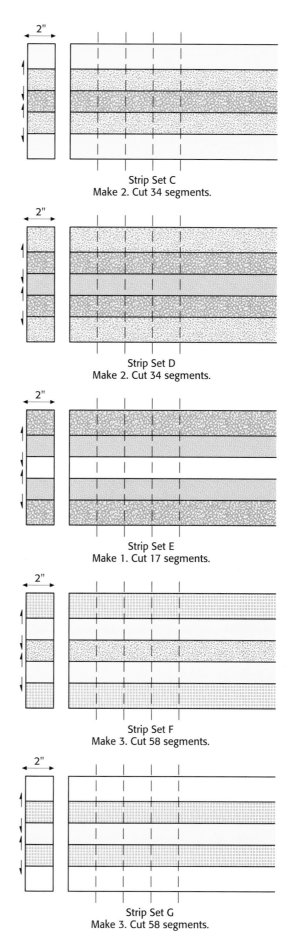

Strip Set C
Make 2. Cut 34 segments.

Strip Set D
Make 2. Cut 34 segments.

Strip Set E
Make 1. Cut 17 segments.

Strip Set F
Make 3. Cut 58 segments.

Strip Set G
Make 3. Cut 58 segments.

3. To make the Sisters blocks, stitch 4 cream 2" squares, 2 light purple 2" squares, 8 cream-and-dark-pink half-square-triangle units, 2 strip set A segments, and 1 strip set B segment together into 5 horizontal rows as shown. Press the seams in the directions indicated. Stitch the rows together. Press the seams in the directions indicated. Make 18.

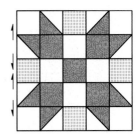

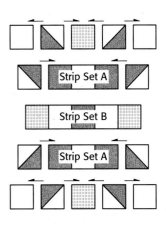

Make 18.

4. To make the Many Trips blocks, stitch 2 strip set C segments, 2 strip set D segments, and 1 strip set E segment together as shown. Press the seams in the directions indicated. Make 17.

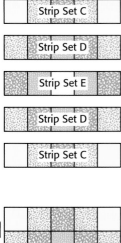

Make 17.

5. To make the sashing units, stitch a strip set F segment to each strip set G segment. Press the seams toward strip set G. Make 58.

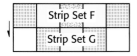

Make 58.

6. To make the block rows, stitch 3 Sisters blocks, 2 Many Trips blocks, and 4 sashing units together as shown. Press the seams toward the sashing units. Make 4 rows. For the alternating rows, stitch 3 Many Trips blocks, 2 Sisters blocks, and 4 sashing units together as shown. Press the seams toward the sashing units. Make 3 rows.

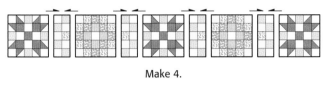

Make 4.

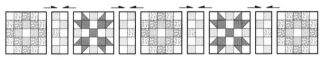

Make 3.

7. To make the sashing rows, stitch 5 sashing units and 4 cream 3½" squares together as shown. Press the seams toward the sashing units. Make 6 rows.

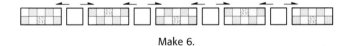

Make 6.

8. Alternately stitch the block rows and sashing rows together as shown.

QUILT FINISHING

Refer to "Finishing Touches" on pages 13–17.

1. Stitch the inner border, then the middle border, and finally the outer border to the quilt-top edges.
2. Layer the quilt top with batting and backing; baste.
3. Quilt as desired.
4. Bind the edges and add a label to the quilt back.

HOT AUGUST NIGHTS

Project instructions begin on page 52.

By Terri Nussbaum, 68" x 86". Quilted by Jeanine Whittington.

If you take one block and change the colors of one of the elements, you can create two different quilts. These two quilts are constructed with the same number of blocks in the same size, but some of the dark fabric fan blades in "Hot August Nights" were exchanged for

SUMMER BREEZE

Project instructions begin on page 54.

By Terri Nussbaum, 69½" x 87½". Quilted by Jeanine Whittington.

background fabric in "Summer Breeze." "Summer Breeze" also introduces a second fan blade fabric, which creates two colors of fans that appear to float across the quilt top.

Hot August Nights

Finished Block Size: 9"
Number of Blocks: 48
Setting: Straight

MATERIALS

Yardage is based on 42" wide fabric.

1⅞ yds. light green print for block backgrounds

2⅞ yds. dark small-scale print for fan blade edges and binding

¼ yd. light purple print for fan centers

2½ yds. dark large-scale print for fan blades and outer border

½ yd. white solid for inner border

½ yd. purple solid for middle border

6 yds. fabric for backing

76" x 94" piece of batting

CUTTING

From the light green print, cut:

4 strips, 1½" x 42"; crosscut the strips into 96 squares, 1½" x 1½", for block backgrounds

8 strips, 5⅞" x 42"; crosscut the strips into 48 squares, 5⅞" x 5⅞". Cut each square once diagonally to yield 96 half-square triangles for block backgrounds.

3 strips, 1⅞" x 42"; crosscut the strips into 48 squares, 1⅞" x 1⅞", for block backgrounds

7 strips, 2" x 42", for inner border

From the dark small-scale print, cut:

8 strips, 9" x 42"; crosscut the strips into 192 strips, 1½" x 9", for fan blade edges

8 strips, 2½" x 42", for binding

From the light purple print, cut:

4 strips, 1½" x 42"; crosscut the strips into 96 squares, 1½" x 1½", for fan centers

From the dark large-scale print, cut:

8 strips, 5⅞" x 42"; crosscut the strips into 48 squares, 5⅞" x 5⅞". Cut each square once diagonally to yield 96 half-square triangles for fan blades.

7 strips, 5" x 42", for outer border

From the white solid, cut:

7 strips, 2" x 42", for inner border

From the purple solid, cut:

7 strips, 1½" x 42", for middle border

QUILT-TOP ASSEMBLY

1. Refer to "Flip-and-Sew Corners" on page 9 to stitch a green 1½" x 1½" square to one end of a dark small-scale print 1½" x 9" strip as shown. Make 96. Repeat with the purple 1½" x 1½" squares and the remaining dark small-scale print 1½" x 9" strips. Make 96.

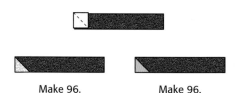

Make 96.   Make 96.

2. With the long raw edges aligned, place a green half-square triangle on a strip from step 1 with a green corner. Extend the end of the triangle ¼" beyond the green corner as shown. With the half-square triangle on the bottom, stitch the pieces together. Press the seam toward the half-square triangle. Trim the end of the strip opposite the green corner even with the edge of the large triangle and at a 45° angle. Make 96 background triangle units. Repeat with the dark large-scale print half-square triangles and the strips from step 1 with a purple corner to make 96 main triangle units.

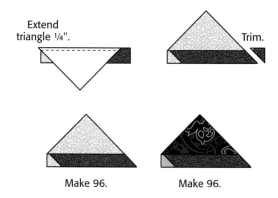

Extend triangle ¼".   Trim.

Make 96.   Make 96.

3. To make the blocks, position a green 1⅞" x 1⅞" square at the point of a main triangle unit as shown, aligning the raw edges. Stitch approximately 1" down the square as shown. Finger-press the seam toward the triangle. Stitch a background triangle unit to the left-hand edge of the unit as shown. Press the seam toward the background triangle unit. Continue in this manner, adding a main triangle unit and then a background triangle unit. Press the seams toward the newest addition. After adding the last triangle unit, go back and stitch the remainder of the first seam. Make 48 blocks.

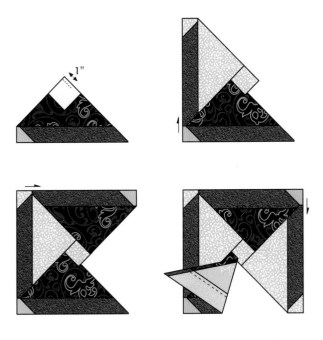

Make 48.

4. Referring to "Assembling the Quilt Top" on page 10, arrange the blocks into 8 horizontal rows of 6 blocks each as shown. Stitch the blocks in each row together. Press the seams in opposite directions from row to row. Stitch the rows together. Press the seams in one direction.

QUILT FINISHING

Refer to "Finishing Touches" on pages 13–17.

1. Stitch the inner border, then the middle border, and finally the outer border to the quilt-top edges.

2. Layer the quilt top with batting and backing; baste.

3. Quilt as desired.

4. Bind the edges and add a label to the quilt back.

Summer Breeze

Finished Block Size: 9"
Number of Blocks: 48
Setting: Straight

MATERIALS

Yardage is based on 42"-wide fabric.

2⅝ yds. cream print for block backgrounds

1⅜ yds. green print for fan blade edges, fan centers, and inner border

⅝ yd. dark pink print for fan blade edges

⅝ yd. black print for fan blade edges

⅝ yd. black print for fan blades

⅞ yd. medium pink print #1 for fan blades

⅝ yd. medium pink print #2 for middle border

2 yds. black floral print for outer border and binding

6 yds. fabric for backing

77" x 95" piece of batting

> *Tip* To create a shadow effect on the fan blades, choose a fabric for the fan edges that is just a shade darker than the fabric used for the blades.

CUTTING

From the cream print, cut:

2 strips, 9" x 42"; crosscut the strips into 48 strips, 1½" x 9", for block backgrounds

10 strips, 5⅞" x 42"; crosscut the strips into 60 squares, 5⅞" x 5⅞". Cut each square once diagonally to yield 120 half-square triangles for block backgrounds.

3 strips, 1½" x 42"; crosscut the strips into 72 squares, 1½" x 1½", for block backgrounds

3 strips, 1⅞" x 42"; crosscut the strips into 48 squares, 1⅞" x 1⅞", for block backgrounds

From the green print, cut:

3 strips, 9" x 42"; crosscut the strips into 72 rectangles, 1½" x 9", for fan blade edges

3 strips, 1½" x 42"; crosscut the strips into 72 squares, 1½" x 1½", for fan centers

7 strips, 1½" x 42", for inner border

From the dark pink print, cut:

2 strips, 9" x 42"; crosscut the strips into 40 rectangles, 1½" x 9", for fan blade edges

From the black print for fan blade edges, cut:

2 strips, 9" x 42"; crosscut the strips into 32 rectangles, 1½" x 9"

From the black print for fan blades, cut:

3 strips, 5⅞" x 42"; crosscut the strips into 16 squares, 5⅞" x 5⅞". Cut each square once diagonally to yield 32 half-square triangles.

From the medium pink print #1, cut:

4 strips, 5⅞" x 42"; crosscut the strips into 20 squares, 5⅞" x 5⅞". Cut each square once diagonally to yield 40 half-square triangles for fan blades.

From the medium pink print #2, cut:

7 strips, 2¼" x 42", for middle border

From the black floral print for outer border and binding, cut:

8 strips, 5½" x 42", for outer border

8 strips, 2½" x 42", for binding

QUILT-TOP ASSEMBLY

1. Refer to "Flip-and-Sew Corners" on page 9 to stitch a cream 1½" x 1½" square to one end of a green 1½" x 9" strip as shown. Make 72. In the same manner, stitch the green 1½" x 1½" squares to the dark pink 1½" x 9" strips as shown. Make 40. Repeat to stitch the remaining green 1½" squares to the black print 1½" x 9" strips. Make 32.

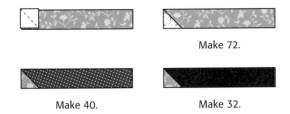

Make 72.

Make 40.

Make 32.

2. With the long raw edges aligned, place a black half-square triangle on a black strip with a green flip-and-sew corner from step 1. Extend the end of the triangle ¼" beyond the flip-and-sew corner as shown. With the half-square triangle on the bottom, stitch the pieces together along the long edges. Press the seam toward the half-square triangle. Trim the end of the strip opposite the flip-and-sew corner even with the edge of the large triangle and

at a 45° angle. Make 32 black triangle units. Repeat with the medium pink #1 half-square triangles and the dark pink strips with green flip-and-sew corners. Make 40. In the same manner, stitch the cream half-square triangles to the green strips with cream flip-and-sew corners. Make 72. Stitch the remaining cream half-square triangles to the cream 1½" x 9" strips. Make 48.

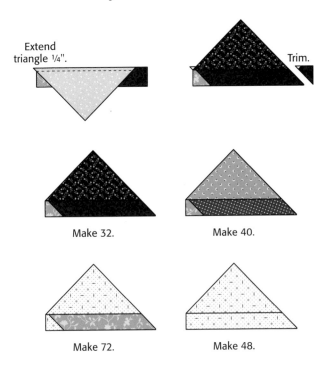

Extend triangle ¼".

Trim.

Make 32.

Make 40.

Make 72.

Make 48.

3. To make the blocks, position a cream print 1⅞" x 1⅞" square at the point of a black triangle unit from step 2 as shown, aligning the raw edges. Stitch approximately 1" down the square as shown. Finger-press the seam toward the triangle. Stitch a cream-and-green triangle unit to the left-hand edge of the unit as shown. Press the seam toward the cream unit. Continue in this manner to add 2 all-cream triangle units. Always press the seam toward the newest addition. After adding the last triangle unit, go back and stitch the remainder of the first seam. Make 12. Follow the block diagrams to make the remaining blocks in the same manner.

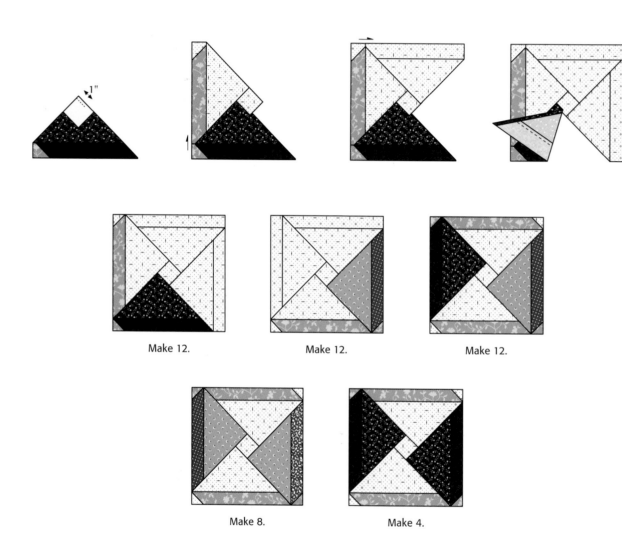

Make 12.

Make 12.

Make 12.

Make 8.

Make 4.

4. Referring to "Assembling the Quilt Top" on page 10, arrange the blocks into 8 horizontal rows of 6 blocks each as shown. Stitch the blocks in each row together. Press the seams in opposite directions from row to row. Stitch the rows together. Press the seams in one direction.

QUILT FINISHING

Refer to "Finishing Touches" on pages 13–17.

1. Stitch the inner border, then the middle border, and finally the outer border to the quilt-top edges.
2. Layer the quilt top with batting and backing; baste.
3. Quilt as desired.
4. Bind the edges and add a label to the quilt back.

THE LEGAL SYSTEM

Project instructions begin on page 60.

By Terri Nussbaum, 54" x 67½". Quilted by Jeanine Whittington.

Color placement within blocks is another way to create changes within a design. Both of these quilts are made up of Courthouse Steps blocks. In "The Legal System," the strips, or logs, that make up the blocks are arranged to create blocks with a scrappy half and a blue half. The blocks are then arranged in rows horizontally and rotated to create the lightning-

GARDEN TILES

Project instructions begin on page 62.

By Terri Nussbaum, 59½" x 70¼". Quilted by Jeanine Whittington.

streak design. In "Garden Tiles," the logs are arranged to make eight different block col-orations. Set diagonally, the blocks produce an intricate design that resembles the garden tiles for which the quilt is named.

The Legal System

MATERIALS

Yardage is based on 42"-wide fabric.

2⅝ yds. blue print for blocks and binding

2⅞ yds. *total* assorted color scraps for blocks

4 yds. fabric for backing

62" x 75" piece of batting

CUTTING

From the blue print, cut:

68 strips, 1¼" x 42"; crosscut 3 strips into 16 strips, 1¼" x 6½", for block center strip sets. Set the remaining strips aside for strip piecing the blocks.

From the assorted scraps, cut:

32 strips, 1¼" x 6½", for block center unit strip sets. Cut the remaining scraps into 1¼" wide strips for strip piecing the blocks.

QUILT-TOP ASSEMBLY

1. To make the block center units, refer to "Strip Sets" on page 8 to stitch 1 blue and 2 assorted scrap 1¼" x 6½" strips together as shown. Press the seams in the directions indicated. Make 16. From the strip sets, cut 80 segments, each 1¼" wide.

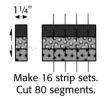

Make 16 strip sets.
Cut 80 segments.

2. To make block A, position 1 block center unit vertically with the blue segment at the top. With the top and long raw edges aligned, stitch an assorted scrap 1¼" strip to the left-hand side of the block center unit (log #1). In the same manner, stitch a blue 1¼" x 42" strip to the right-hand side of the unit (log #2). Press the seams toward the new strips. Trim the strip ends even with the bottom of the unit.

Following the piecing order diagram, continue adding strips in the order indicated. Use the blue strips for logs #3, #6, #7, #10, #11, and #14; and the assorted scrap strips for logs #4, #5, #8, #9, #12, and #13. Always press the seams toward the new strip and trim the strip ends before adding another strip. Make 40.

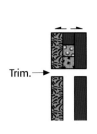
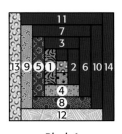

Block A
Make 40.

3. Referring to step 2, use the remaining block center units to make block B. Use the blue strips for logs #1, #4, #5, #8, #9, #12, and #13; and the assorted scrap strips for logs #2, #3, #6, #7, #10, #11, and #14. Make 40.

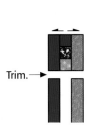
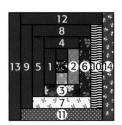

Block B
Make 40.

4. Referring to "Assembling the Quilt Top" on page 10, arrange the blocks into 10 horizontal rows of 8 blocks each, alternating the positions of blocks A and B from row to row and rotating them as shown. Stitch the blocks in each row together. Press the seams in opposite directions from row to row. Stitch the rows together. Press the seams in one direction.

QUILT FINISHING

Refer to "Finishing Touches" on pages 13–17.

1. Layer the quilt top with batting and backing; baste.
2. Quilt as desired.
3. Bind the edges and add a label to the quilt back.

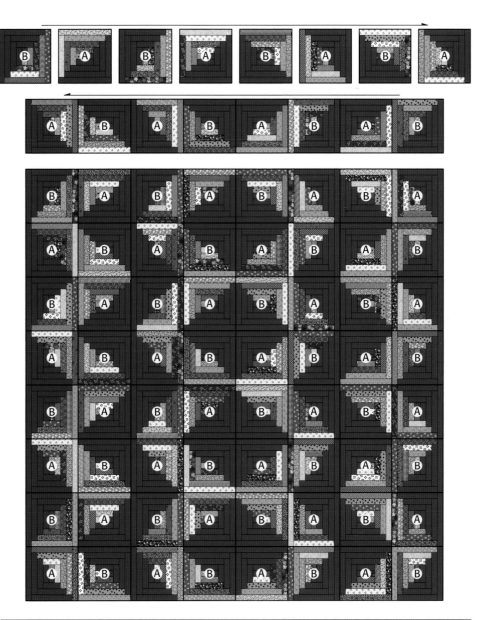

Tip *Each time you add a new log, it should cross 2 seams. If it does not, you have added the log to the wrong side.*

Garden Tiles

Finished Block Size: 6¾"
Number of Blocks: 60
Setting: Diagonal

MATERIALS

Yardage is based on 42"-wide fabric.

2⅛ yds. dark brown print for blocks and setting triangles

¾ yd. medium green print for blocks

¾ yd. dark floral print for blocks

¾ yd. beige print for blocks

¾ yd. light gold print for blocks

½ yd. red print for blocks and binding

4¼ yds. fabric for backing

67" x 78" piece of batting

CUTTING

From the dark brown print, cut:

36 strips, 1¼" x 42"; crosscut 2 strips into 42 squares, 1¼" x 1¼", for block center units. Set the remaining strips aside for strip piecing the blocks.

2 strips, 13" x 42"; crosscut the strips into 6 squares, 13" x 13". Cut each square twice diagonally to yield 24 side setting triangles (you will use 22 and have 2 left over).

1 square, 8½" x 8½"; cut the square once diagonally to yield 2 corner setting triangles

From the medium green print, cut:

17 strips, 1¼" x 42"; crosscut 1 strip into 10 squares, 1¼" x 1¼", for block center units. Set the remaining strips aside for strip piecing the blocks.

From the dark floral print, cut:

17 strips, 1¼" x 42"; crosscut 1 strip into 10 squares, 1¼" x 1¼", for block center units. Set the remaining strips aside for strip piecing the blocks.

From the beige print, cut:

21 strips, 1¼" x 42"; crosscut 2 strips into 49 squares, 1¼" x 1¼", for block center units. Set the remaining strips aside for strip piecing the blocks.

From the light gold print, cut:

21 strips, 1¼" x 42"; crosscut 2 strips into 49 squares, 1¼" x 1¼", for block center units. Set the remaining strips aside for strip piecing the blocks.

From the red print, cut:

14 strips, 1¼" x 42"; crosscut 1 strip into 20 squares, 1¼" x 1¼", for block center units. Set the remaining strips aside for strip piecing the blocks.

QUILT-TOP ASSEMBLY

1. Referring to the block diagrams on page 63, stitch 3 squares, each 1¼" x 1¼" together to make the center units. Make 60.

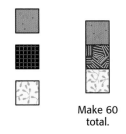

Make 60 total.

2. Referring to the block diagrams on page 63 and the piecing order diagram, stitch the appropriate color 1¼" x 42" strip for logs #1 and #2 to each side of the block center units. Press the seams toward the new strips. Trim the strips even with the ends of the block center unit. Continue adding the appropriate color 1¼" strips for each block in the order indicated. Always press the seams toward the new strip and trim the strip ends before adding another strip. Make 20 each of blocks A and B, 4 each of blocks C and E, 5 each of blocks D and F, and 1 each of blocks G and H.

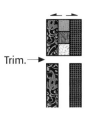

Trim. →

3. Referring to "Assembling the Quilt Top" on page 10, arrange the blocks and side setting triangles into 11 diagonal rows, positioning each block as shown. Stitch the blocks and side setting triangles in each row together. Press the seams in opposite directions from row to row. Stitch the rows together. Add the corner setting triangles. Press the seams in one direction. Trim the edges of the quilt top so they are straight.

Block A
Make 20.

Block B
Make 20.

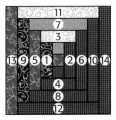

Block C
Make 4.

Block D
Make 5.

Block E
Make 4.

Block F
Make 5.

Block G
Make 1.

Block H
Make 1.

QUILT FINISHING

Refer to "Finishing Touches" on pages 13–17.

1. Layer the quilt top with batting and backing; baste.
2. Quilt as desired.
3. Bind the edges and add a label to the quilt back.

About the Author

Terri Nussbaum grew up in the beautiful apple country of Wenatchee, Washington. At an early age, Terri fell in love with the color, texture, and feel of fabric. During visits at their great-grandmother's, Terri and her sisters kept themselves entertained with the fabric scraps from their great-grandmother's scrap bag. Terri's mother was a beautiful seamstress, but Terri inherited her love for quilting from both her great-grandmother and grandmother.

After moving to the Seattle area in 1974, Terri began quilting and taking classes. Soon she was hooked and began teaching classes herself at local quilt shops. Terri continues to teach at various quilt shops, quilting retreats, and area quilting guilds. Four times a year, Terri hosts "Piecing in the Pines," a quilting retreat at Lake Easton Resort in the Cascade Range of Washington State.

Terri is married to Brian and they have a teenager, Rusty. Together they enjoy snowmobiling, skiing, and camping with their RV travel club.